~~Being~~ Helpful

nnabel Spenceley
el Underwood

E BOOKS

A Cherrytree book

Designed and produced by
A S Publishing

First published 1997
by Cherrytree Press Ltd
a subsidiary of
The Chivers Company Ltd
Windsor Bridge Road
Bath BA2 3AX

British Library Cataloguing in Publication Data
Amos, Janine
    Being Helpful. – (Growing Up)
    1. Helpful behaviour – Juvenile literature
    I. Title
    302.1'4

    ISBN 0 7451 5305 4 (hardcover)
    ISBN 0 7540 9016 7 (softcover)

Printed in Malaysia

Joseph and Li

It's tidy-up time.

"Let's put everything back. Then we'll be able to find it tomorrow," says Dave.

Joseph puts the bricks back
in the box.

Li puts the dough in the tub.

Li finds a brick in the dough.
He takes it to Joseph.

Joseph has packed all the bricks
away.

Li is still busy.
What could Joseph do?

Joseph goes over to Li.
"I can help you now," he says.

They clear up the rest of the
dough together.

"We've finished!" says Joseph.

"You worked together," says
Dave. "You helped each other."

Harry and Rosie

"Waah!" Rosie is crying.

"She's been crying all night!" sighs Mum.

"Do you want your rattle, Rosie?"
asks mum.

"Nah!" says Rosie.

"Do you want your bottle, Rosie?"
asks Mum.

"Nah!" says Rosie.

"Brrr! Brrr!" goes the telephone.
"Waah!" cries Rosie.

"Oh, no!" sighs Mum.
How does Mum feel?

Harry goes over to Rosie.

He makes a funny face.

Rosie smiles.

Harry wiggles his fingers.

Rosie laughs.

Harry laughs too. "She's happy
now," says Harry.

"Thanks, Harry," smiles Mum.

"You helped Rosie – and that helped me."

Sometimes people need help.
Perhaps you can do something to
make things better.
Or you may need to ask how you
can help.

You might want help yourself
if you have a problem.
Who could you ask to help you?